The Bosses

Sebastian Agudelo

saturnalia books

Distributed by University Press of New England
Hanover and London

Saturnalia Books
105 Woodside Rd.
Ardmore, PA 19003
info@saturnaliabooks.com

ISBN: 978-0-9899797-4-0
Library of Congress Control Number: 2017937894

Book Design by Saturnalia Books
Printing by McNaughton & Gunn
Cover Art: William Etty, Candaules, King of Lydia Shews his Wife by Stealth to Gyges

Author Photo: K. Mach

Distributed by:
University Press of New England
1 Court Street
Lebanon, NH 03766
800-421-1561

Thanks to the editors of the following journals for publishing some of this poems, sometimes in different versions: *The Nation*: "Mugwump," "Myth" (as "Therianthrope,") "In Shape"; *The Cortland Review*: "You Tube Poem," "Folk"; *The Burnside Review:* "The OCD Poem," "The Cure"; *Scoundrel Time*: "The History of Wrongs"; *Tikkun Magazine*: "Of Biblical Proportions."

for Madeleine and Katharina

Table of Contents

Yes, these business people have great energy. There's a question as to what is burned to produce it and what things we can and can't burn.
—Saul Bellow

Jesus, make haste to save us
from all those smug, nasty, overpaid, with dumb
nicknames, who would see us depart and be no more.

—Karen Solie

Mugwump

O beggar, bigwig, mugwump
—W.H. Auden

If you got to look it up, don't use it.
A pity since we've all known one:
guy checking time cards, signing requisitions,
woman working her way center stage
of my worries. Every decision she weighs,
I'm on the balance, the bigwig.
Turns out, as from the mess of history,
because the Algonquians
had no clue about *Imperator*
and Centurion, and seeing no way
to excise dominion and ranks from the account,
giving Caesar what's Caesar's so to speak,
and Antiochus the Seleucid's also, John Eliot,
to let his catechumens into the kindling of the lord,
his Praying Indians in Natick, Ponkipog, Lowell,
rendered the smug of sovereign, war-lord, arrayer
in a single Wampanoag word, come down
as *Mugwump*, dated but still chiefly American
in its broad-brush picture of the nothings
who oversaw our stints at register or sink,
or the guy tightening the barmaid's dirndl
or mid-level manager
and CEO too. They're fine, I figure,
with our menial seasons, the bosses
seeing us cross over—shrugs of resignation—
from knuckle down to knuckle under
and since acquaintance with the eternal
requires no minutiae, lives by mass and matins,
Mugwump serves their kind right.

Late Capital

Not the graffiti on the delivery docks
of the boarded factory, though a detective
on TV insists the cedilla-like squiggle
points to a turf war with a body count.

Nor the stuff that was assembled there:
dome lounges, the Pioneer Zephyr;
and less so the ex-owner, mogul, titan,
put to pasture by the boys in M&A.

Not the irony of kids off the vocational high
a block away, their dare do's, fights,
regroupings, throwing rocks to break
another pane like Luddites come too late.

The archeological footprint with tracks
of Rent-a-Fence sandbagged every length
as if to keep for the new settlers who never come
a carious hulk at sunset, our *Götterdämmerung*.

Urban Renewal

When the surveyors arrive
with theodolites and transits,
you know destruction is total,
as in no one has kicked stuff
out of the way in years,
so this, investor knows,
is no bad place to park
money for a while,
let markets settle.
The demo crew will come
sort brick from metal, haul it.
When the lot is furrowed
planners move their clipboards
and drawings to the mobile office.
Their ideas have people in them.
So like overfed apparatchiks
risen through ranks,
they rally around the certainty
of blueprints and projections,
the pro forma's make-believe
with its parks and stores,
its low density housing,
a dry-walled land of behest.
The trouble with utopias
is the trouble in us.
Baudelaire is taking a stab at it
bewildered by Haussmann's Paris,
bedeviled by a runway cob.
Augustine is going at it too
though his vantage point

is at the hearth, under
the nursing covers.
Doctor, Bishop, Berber Saint,
he is obsessed with breasts
and suck, to him the hub,
the nerve center to the domestic.
He's going, how he wailed,
how he saw a child rage
at the sight of brother nursing.
What if tantrum outlives its purpose?
What if it abides, like sediment
latches to mantle and pearls
into the sort that would bring
calamities down on Rome?
He is down to the *root of evil*,
untangling the radicle of hunger
from the xylem of *amour prope*
and has a point: Who can tell
among the people out there?
If investor is anything to go by,
off his Jaguar to squinny at tract,
subsidized, in profit's now,
the future of CAD printouts
trusting no eraser marks.
He's here with a shovel
to break ground and bask
in the photo op, sure enough
as ruddy and pampered
as a baby latched to nipple.

In Shape

Here are the old folks anchored by old wisdom
to the ground, or by old wisdom swiveling
on one foot and deliberately tracing a camber
in the horizon, karate chop by karate chop.
So many meticulous minutes into this,
if no castles in the air, they've outlined
that curvilinear ebb and flow in one of Gehry's
pipe dreams: receding chambers, curls, soft arches
cantilevers, like canvases unfolding to wind.
The dog stops dead on its tracks, sits
and gives a slant look that's all dog candor
and nosiness. The embarrassed owner pulls.
The jogger wrapped in cellophane turns also.
Pure formalists, they are, the old folks,
focusing on the movement of an ostensible
shape, a structure, something wrought within
and needing outing, though it's nothing like art,
just fending off stuff inside: cancers, heart attacks
in slow-mo, real moves of fight and war.

The Philadelphia Sound

Nothing to write about:
Man and "Lyrical God,"
how he christened the contrivance
clobbered to mimic the school desk
where he learned.
He sets it up by the exit,
makes the black acrylic sheets
rattle, babble, reverb
with his forearm, a pen, spoons.
A bunch of wannabes gang around
turfing a bit, mouthing the chorus.
The drill team in the median
could for auxetic purposes
bring it on, have a showdown,
upgrade the sort of off-kilter
stichomythia of tunes
Ives stitched together
from corners to score
who we were, reconcile
shark, braggart, brawler,
the pious, the patriotic,
the slatterns and the boss.
They trail off though, no team
per se, a quad, two quints, bass
with plastic collection jars
taped to each drum.
Born of necessity or budget cuts,
the kids with feathers on their hats,
duct-taped drumheads;
some music of necessity also:
sea shanty, waulking song, lullaby,
like a live cinder smuggled

from the gods to make it through.
And it galled the heart inside him
when he saw the far seen glory of fire
among mortal people.
Pay them no mind. However hard,
the powers that be will be.
Check the guy who claims
he's "Little Sonny"
of *The Intruders* fame,
Gamble & Huff's first moneymakers,
and forefather to *The Stylistics,*
Harold Melvin and the Blue Notes.
No him, no *Love Train,*
Me and Mrs. Jones, Back Stabbers.
Daily, he backs his mobility scooter
against the corner of the bank,
unstraps his prosthetic –
part of his set up—
the leg he props a Solo cup on,
the Roland street amp, the guitar.
Grating, what he does to repertoire.
Ain't No Stopping Us Now,
Only the Strong Survive,
masterpieces some.
What Gamble wrought:
the Philadelphia sound,
the man on the scooter,
the payola scandal,
15 gold singles, 22 gold albums,
him addressing the Republican convention
in a dark suit and topi,
fourteen million dollars worth of hits,

counting every penny.
As I said, not much to write about,
though the amputee is lying,
"Little Sonny" jumped off a bridge in '95.

You Tube Poem

My eight year old is not listening
the baroque high-sass, its gobby fiorituras.
Madeleine is going on about the hair,
a clip on, a weave, a wig, it can't be hers,
the tangled beehive, its cocktail umbrellas.
Then it's Cynthia, and the "Daddy's girl" tat,
the horseshoe and the topless pinup.
Those A-side, boy-crush, *billets doux*
tempered, you'd think, by third wave women's lib
or what it left the public housing gum-molls
loitering around skate parks smoking.
My daughter is not listening.
I skip the ring-side, lurid clips
the fall in Recife, the booing in Belgrade
do Gastonbury, Somerset house, BBC instead.
She's in an orange dress crouching for a sip.
Madeleine wants to know what's in the cup.
I nudge her to the screen, it's the one where snare
yields to bass drum and she mumbles
an homage to the Shangri-Las
before her chorus boys pick it up
scup back and forth kicking thin air.
Now it's décolletage Madeleine cares about
since she's spilling out of some tartan top
or will do a runabout on stage
to pull herself back in a pailleted strapless thing,
jokes *how long it takes to get a dress on*
how quickly it comes off and moves on to some ska.
Kid won't listen. She's deciphering
the pop-up banner for a twelve step program
to the mewls, scats, falsettos
a mannerist one night stand, then the rehab song.

The Daddy Poem

would have me coo, goo, gurgle to echolalia
by the changing table, standing by the crib.
It'll let her rat claw down my shirt, up my sleeve.
It would shackle me to every Rainbow Loom
motif. "One only." "Which one do you want?
Fish-tail, hex-fish, zippy chains?"
"They sound like tortures," I say.
"Just pick," she huffs.
The daddy poem should fear Lear,
shunt Lacan at the lectern punning
le nom du père / the non du père
and his offspring, the tenure-track brood
scurrying like press after scandal
to file copy on the nonsense earns their keep.
One trouble with authority:
you're so over your head the predicate
is all wrong, over the top, i.e. the verb is swat.
As in, I swat the score, literally swat
the middle G to be precise
so Madeleine look up, name the note.
She's whimpers, "Never seen it before."
And do I sentinel or hover as I time her
because if the cage is not cleaned
(five minutes) I'll find her pet a new home?
One day I'll kill the rat.
A friend is sure there are more worrisome
emblems for what troubles authority might rain.
He's talking first hand experience—
his childhood's *nons du père*,
the kind that tindered addictions,
made sister marry, brother buy
a one way trip to just to be haunted still.

Imago? *Pater familias*? Afflatus?
A father on wingchair to crumble self esteem.
I'm filling in. He will not say a word.
I've seen Madeleine check whether I approve.
The voice that troubles authority
has me nurse a pinkie with a pipette,
fiddling with appendages for the critter trail
elbows, tubes, a lookout. Not what kid wants.
She throws tantrum, goes at my shirt.
"More sinned against than sinning,"
Lear in certainty to the storm.
The daddy is in awe of echolalia,
will echolocate the goings-on behind
closed doors but will have no one cry.
Empty threats, shove the cage,
slam the lid, kick toys out of the way
and "you put yourself to bed tonight."
So daddy poem lets mommy in,
striding up the stairs, "what now?"
The whole household goes into a fit.
Kid's beside herself "she's dying, she's dying"
and indeed Flo, the albino rat…
The poem had me slam the lid on it—
go dread what loose ends will loom.
Yeah, for once loom is the right verb.
My friend's father flying LAX to PHL,
downgraded to cargo casting a permanent
shadow. Ask him tell you why,
he's like one of those twitchy guys
by half-lit entryways, on the lam, in noire.
And Lear. Dumb Lear? Bad Lear? At the end
all he wants is someone to undo his button.

The OCD poem

Nothing will get past it, the sills,
the shelves, the books, the table.
It has its epic catalogs, contains
no multitude, winnows instead
fays, holds its hands up
like a surgeon after scrubbing
and begs not to be touched.
Won't listen to reason to stay clean.
It has its exorcist-like moments.
Kid writhes; parents dodge
blobs of conditioner she hurls
because we cut her shower short
and she hasn't worked her way
through a flotilla of soaps
she's docked on the tub's rim,
each dedicated to a body part.
She suds her nostrils, eyelids.
It's my daughter's kicks that start
the OCD poem into being
with all its proscriptions and lists.
Verboten: doorknobs, keyboards
all but a single chair we switch.
She notices it and switches it back.
Check also: museums, subway,
the library and its holdings, dolls.
The OCD poem can't help but list,
has its registers, its enumerations,
its sortings, but we'd be damned
to understand its rationale,
a logic to its odds and ends, despite
the books, *The Meaning of Anxiety*—
a mush of existential musings—

Anxiety Disorders and Phobias—
its dreadful APA prose—
and *Obsessive Children*
with case histories, a cast
of kids from the early seventies.
They'd be my slightly older friends now.
Eric D with his brown eyes and smile.
Herb M, odd looking, tic ridden,
worried about grades and God.
Elvis K, seven, wetting his pants.
Others hit closer home. Mulish,
parsimonious block loners,
who clip travel ads, keep a scrapbook.
The museum pieces of the odd,
difficult to watch, doting on robots
and make believe machines, cornered
in locker rooms. Difficult also,
the explanations' Freudian cargo,
the unconscious forms of hatred,
its *Cherchez la femme.*
A friend writes back, *nowadays*
they have ways of dealing with
the stuff that's crippled us for life,
some consolation. He's right
if what he means is I could use
at least five out of six
What-to-do Guides for Kids
as I still grumble, worry,
can't sleep, am still nail biting.
Madeleine's is *What-to-do*
When Your Brain Gets Stuck
and it takes her on a mental tour

throughout the house to itemize
the contents of the garbage cans
and then imagine what if
we didn't rid ourselves from junk.
The eggshells, the cans and cartons
are piling over toy and teddy bear.
The cat's bewildered as it traipses
through the litter, a metaphor
for her brain unable to sort out
a valid thought from junk and junk
jamming every move with *germs,*
dirt, unlocked doors, check, maker sure...
like a speaker in a new language
hems and stutters and hesitates.
She gets it but will still cleanse
herself raw with dish detergent.
The OCD poem is clean, its folds
pin-tucked, but it's not without
its humorous asides. She drinks,
after all, only from a Martini glass,
does not so much air dry as
jump-jack herself dry. Oh, Forgot,
verboten: towels, her bed, pajamas.
Her bedroom's like an abductee's,
the sort of clock-stopped-here
ground zero, Pompeiish aftermath
with Kit and Molly and Sage left mid-play
as evidence a child was there.
No iPhone, no iPad, no books.
We are compiling our own lists
mea culpas, maps of the genome,
also the tableaux we'll flesh out,
answer as thoroughly as possible
for the clinic's questionnaire,
a fourteen double-sided page

affair with fill-in the boxes, rank.
Do you think your child is weird?
Has he/she set things on fire?
Kid spitting, kid clawing, kid hitting.
Kid fretting, frozen,
unable to find a surface in our room
to lay her clothes down, two hours;
kid draping every surface to sit.
Mother also goes ballistic, bags
kid's entire wardrobe, drives it
to goodwill. Kid spits and claws
again. One night neighbors
call the cops on us...
The disaster area of the pure type
writes Ugazio. T*he disaster area*
of perfect harmony. The impossible
perfect life which brings destruction.
That's one way of putting it.
The capaciousness of catalog:
cemeteries, her friend, airports,
used soap, her hairbrush, shoes,
the dollhouse, the embargoed life
where action halts but the larger
story brews, the one that births
ritual, sacrifice, ceremony,
the abominations of Leviticus,
enmities and clan and bomb,
where miasma and catharsis hold
and steer us the way magnetic field
does bird when cold turns bitter.

The Cure

The cure begins with lists, a mason jar
and poker chips which kid will earn and spend.
It's sweets on demand, outing to the Shake Shack
and for two chips she can buy fifteen minutes
of radio time and have me sing along
to Katie Perry, Taio Cruz, Taylor Swift.
Dr. says the tics might morph to Tourettes.
The cure has po-mo sensibilities, jettisons
the canon I compiled to understand
what frets her to a standstill, her double jeopardy.
Dr. will have none of that, none of Tillich's forces:
"the depth of us, the judge who is oneself
and stands against oneself." None of that.
Impractical *tristia*, as good as camphor.
We are team Madeleine now.
Dr. is coach, with pep talks for the child
and we cheer along that OCD won't win.
The cure mines Japan and now,
hoards Iwako erasers, Daruma dolls,
sushi and teeth pencil toppers.
There are tamagotchi apps
if she doesn't hold her breath or wash hands;
if she wears the same pajamas three nights in a row,
rubber hedgehogs or parkabears.
Pufferfish and Maneki-nekos,
our only currency or hope
to rid the kid from whatever dug its heels
in her. We have twenty sessions.
The cure is time sensitive.
Dr. wants the plush toys she did away with
and she bets two dollars Madeleine can balance

the stuffed armadillo two minutes on her nose.
They are filming through the one way mirror.
Dr. pays up. The cure is capital, capitalist,
feet on the ground with enough leverage
to quell what voice whispers unrest,
the judge who is oneself and is against oneself
which is our black ice and silence.
The cure will have none of that.
Its excess sweets, its cheese fries, malts,
its catchy tunes and cheers will make it work
whatever the cause might be. Madeleine
doesn't know, we asked, she doesn't know.

Petit Bourgeois

...the petit bourgeois, for whom the production of commodities is the ne
plus ultra of human freedom and individual independence...
—Das Capital

And the superflux is real, no doubt,
the party favors, bagged on the table,
gewgaws from the dollar store or Chinatown,
the pro forma, largely middle class
"*embarrass de richesse*"
ready to go strew or clutter
someone else's family room,
however much we patch it
paycheck-to-paycheck
haunted by tuition, sleepless over
fees, braces, piano lessons.
There's a list of chores still to get done.
Madeleine splits, texts me from her room
her bitmoji avatar, the caption this time:
"The struggle is real."
We've got yet to pick balloons, paper plates
and don't forget the dog food.
In a bit the kids will sort of stunt
themselves like she who couldn't help
look at burning plain, at what God would.
"No more a woman, not yet quite a stone."
A roomful of children has nothing
to do with Pentateuchal cataclysms.
The parents would not approve.
They trust us, drop their kids
and instructions, diets, allergies,

designated SPF's, haul in gifts.
In this party game, a roomful
of children freeze mid-pose
as exhibits to a different museum
each go-round and we, the grown-ups,
try to catch them if they blink
or smirk or gesture and they tell us
what or who they are.
We have a dummy flashlight
like in the movie they learned this from.
First hot dogs, cake, open the gifts
a recycle bin full of packaging
and gift-wrap, the side-effect
or spillover of the ne plus ultra
of human freedom, pace Marx,
or individual independence.
No need to bring the class thing in
and certainly don't involve the kids.
In the Triassic, boys are lizard-hip
carnivores mid-pounce
and each blurts names of fossils
unearthed in the lagerstätte
or Liaoning. We, the parents,
wouldn't know. They pored
through books. Some had tie-ins,
dig-a-dinos, another Edu-Toy.
There's also Ents and Orcs on one go,
the most recondite fauna, stuff
from d'Aulerie: mini-Minervas in mock
intractable scowls, a Poseidon astride
a stairwell, Hermes balancing on one foot

holding up a make-believe caduceus.
Well travelled, pampered, precocious,
our kids know their Greeks, like Romans
yes, in the sort of Rome where scion's at the helm
and there is zero wiggle or elbow room.
"The struggle is real" to quote avatar.
The kids, our kids freeze, no burning plain,
lots of knowledge, but as if a little lost.

As the Generations of…

Not yet the amnesiac Neverland
where chia pets gambol on night stands
in that last known address: assisted living.
But not far, the background and interface
of videogames my mother spends hours on
to keep her memory spruce. She's ending
where Madeleine begins, with bloated
animatrons skittering prompt to prompt,
word problems too--she adds, substracts,
the grouping in Venn diagrams,
click and drag and drop, tree is to earth
as star is to...right answer is open sesame
to new levels the kid learns, grandma
is just rehearsing not to forget
with her alarms to tell the times for pills
and drops, the color coded organizer,
a calendar with staggered boxes
for each daily dose, like 3-D bar graphs
to track aches. And where's the cane?
Madeleine was playing with it.
I can't tell where I am in this poem,
I have my own alarms jing
somewhere in the tricks of generations,
with leaves blowing every which way.
Propping my mother by the arm,
holding the kid's hand, I look both ways.

Playfields

la sconoscente vita che i fé sozza
ad ogne conoscenza or li fa bruni.
— Dante, *Inferno* VII

They replaced the sign overnight,
rid the flight by white out
on the NO, the decal of a shaggy

labradoodle on the backslash circle
that kept dog walkers out. Kids,
up to mischief, I'm sure, the dreadlocky

white boys on a skateboard
culture jamming here, yarn bombing
elsewhere. But facilities can't risk

mixed signals. The playfields,
empty for the most part,
unwithered in drought, are watered

by a rig school screws to fire hydrant,
and if indeed things are as they seem
and the sprinklers are scattering

unmetered municipal resources,
a dog owner might make a call.
The dads, VP and V.I.P's, rush in

mid-afternoon trying to steal
from the frowst of boardrooms
a few hours, come see the kids,

step outside the sticky hives
of organizational charts. From where I stand,
outside the fence, they are bad fortune's

functionaries carrying her hard choices
bit by bit, pink slips, marching orders,
slaps on the wrist, smack on the face,

or I can't see them otherwise somehow
if the car makes are anything to go by.
The unconscionable life that taints them

makes them undistinguished, undistiguishable,
ad ogne conoscenza or li fa bruni.
Something like that, pacing the side lines

at warm up, red faced on their phones,
red faced on the bleachers, goading their kid,
calling on coach or referee.

They must've had childhoods somewhere
and now they remember nothing of their lives,
or else the humiliation scurffed

and made them hard as nails.
I've seen them drop their kids
in the morning, hunched under backpacks

bulging with curricula, after-school
appurtenances dangling like tackle
from loops and latch, puntero cleats,

tennis racquets, guitar or violin all on one child.
Anyway, no mutts in their courts.
Make no mistake, this is no level playfield.

Mexicans descend on it with a small fleet
of mowers, weed-wackers, leaf-blowers
off a flat-truck just to vanish in the otherworld

that's the unaccounted half of Exodus,
the sinewy side of Disaporas.
They patch divots with sod rolls,

trim the edges to the fence, two stroke engine
strapped to they back, the price of admission,
so the kids after school come kick the ball.

They run like the liberal imagination
healthy, guileless, burdened with tradition
and do not go taunt or look them the wrong way.

The parents will take measures, just look
at the Mexicans today, unrolling a wind screen
to zip tie to fence, cover the children,

for when they warm up for the game.
You can imagine the motion introduced
by the red faced parent at the PTA.

They need a little privacy, guarding a bit more
to be curtained, as if caught *in flagrante*
or mid-indecency, part of a cover-up.

Myth

As with exuviae burring to the bark

minotaur had to have a live animal as source

and hunger, the moil that attends the kill

and props beast near night start,

lets it squat in dream to mix and match

till monster mitigates unease.

Enter King, husband, father

ready to co-opt, adopt, foster.

He'll dream a decoy, strap it to the wife,

awe with labyrinth and cash-in

on mooncalf, exacter, changeling,

the horror, the first puppet of the state.

The Birth of History
(after Herodotus)

what can these long-ago misfortunes tell us of ourselves, of life—
—August Kleinzahler

I.

Nightly he feels her up, fucks her maybe.
Nightly, he can't believe his luck,
welters in a post-coital second-guess:
Is she for real? Is she beautiful?

He rolls over on his back,
gasps for metaphor. *Her shoulders?*
Soft white mist blown from the ocean.
Not half bad, the metaphor that is,

interesting if a wee awry.
One of the guys, you'd think,
with what's going through his mind.
The small of her back?

As if he scored at a singles bar,
reached over for a smoke. *Her neck?*
Moonlight cutting through eucalyptus.
Feel free to recoil from man and similes,

their cuddly, nuzzling residue
groping for the certitude of affiance, troth.
Candaules, after all, is king
and king is something to recoil from

since king can't have uncertainty,
no double-edge, nor overlaps
between one night and marriage,
murder and constitutional convention.

II.

History is being born,
bred out of love, shiver of the loin
or some convulsion went through the walls
to keep man rankling long enough

but enter stage left—as poem
peeks into habit and habitat—
stage left, my ten year old.
"What are you reading?"

She is vis-à-vis Candaules
at the other end of the spectrum
a notional gloaming,
the dusky bat-light end of chronologies

with cranes stopped mid-construction,
not that she knows or cares.
"What are you reading?"
No need go into the indelicate detail,

the concupiscence of potentate,
the bedroom farce about to ensue.
The DSM-IV common axis I
disorder developing before our eyes.

Solon's wise bit that you'd be best
to steer clear of the word happiness
—some caveat, the law giver gives—
will earn at best some mock gang salute

as would the stock-in-trade
"how the mighty fall" that's gimcrack
to the plot. Xerxes and excess and empire?
The "father of history" spiel? "Daddy?"

III.

Parenting: teach or bowdlerize
or figure where to start.
History, born with ants the size of foxes,
dog headed men, gold-digging ants

and bestiary is the least of it
considering a twenty plus page index
from Abae to Zopyrus and a whole lot
of unpronounceables in between,

like tagged specimens on hold
in knowledge's dry storage rooms.
Put another way, go Google for weeks.
Abae: north east corner of Phocis,

famous for an oracle.
Psammis' digital footprint is nil.
He clings from oblivion by a single
mention in the book and his son

Apries isn't Apries either
but a made up name which might be
another way people fit forgetting.
For the kid, I stick with outlandish.

The Gyzantes smeared in red paint
eating monkeys, your stock-in-trade
headless men, eyes in their breast,
though Zopyrus is more interesting.

IV.

"Persian nobleman" Wikipedia says.
Agent provocateur? Fake outcast?
He self-mutilates, crosses enemy lines,
begs for mercy (King cut him up,

he claims) and once he's in,
betrays his host and hands Darius
Babylon on a plate, literal Babylon that is.
One more intrigue pinched out of Homer

but getting a shorthand croquis
of how self-serving scrubber
sneaks and fawns around mighthand,
hedges his bets, steers,

rooster-tails his way to promotion.
I've seen their lessers beeline reception
to graze near the Provost. I'd tell my kid,
these are unexceptional—no dog headed men—

monsters of a kind nonetheless,
lump suckers to Leviathan
and Leviathan is no mythical fish,
"the mortall God," sovereign, grandee.

Value them as you will,
we're conditional clauses
to their dealings. Though *exeunt*
Madeleine happened a while back.

V.

She is due to reappear,
humming Adele or Taylor Swift.
"The veracity of this story is debatable"
says Wikipedia and yet lists Zopyrus

in the external links for Iranian
military commanders
past the Sassians down to the Quds.
Who isn't after all—history being born

and history being history—
in that disoriented, who's who.
The thing is hard-wired for subterfuge,
has its blindfolds, smoke and mirrors,

trap doors, bugs, tattletales
go sort out milestone from aside,
progress from the ways it clears its throat.
Downed passenger jet, slashed jobs,

cease fire, what push notifications
pile up on the lock screen on your phone:
tornado, coups, obit, are a little like maps
in tourist traps with their you're HERE.

Thought HERE is no ontological exercise
but passing quickly, the HERE
with the franchises switching the signs on,
the thing the town enshrines we came to see,

the posters from last week's elections still up,
go figure what part of HERE
will be in the test come time franchise closes.
Abaris? Zeuxidamus? Zancle? Abdera?

VI.

The disclaimers and corrections,
the *testis unus testis nullus* thing,
the liars who might have witnessed the scene
and throng that will not go on record.

Who'd want to as history's notables
are on the rise always. Its Attilas
and Idi Amins. But not so quick.
First, History has a guy

talking about the wife, no joke,
but not unlike one either.
Candaules, the morning after
still wilsome, mulling buttock

or calf, and is he right?
Not that it matters but it does
as it's to become a headline of sorts
despite taking root in the bedstead,

wedlock, family, also known as
the day-to-day, workman-like
version of more lofty uncertainties—
Descartes' wax, Heidegger's blossoms.

Add things to do, a kingdom to run
and others on the stage bringing
their shifty moods and whatnots,
ergo cogito is more a general dunno.

The small of her back?
Here's the *testis unus* thing.
So Candaules turns to Gyges, his slave
and confidant in hopes he'll reassure.

VII.

The fuzz on nape? The hollow behind knee?
Gyges does what slave does, nods,
ahas but isn't slavish enough
to the master's "look at me

then look at her, then look at me again."
Hell-bent, unabashed, as masters are,
he'll have nothing but slave's awe,
will bully him to go crouch

behind a door and spy on queen undressing
leaving, admittedly, little room
for *such hands, the glint of shoulder blade.*
This is history, its very birth,

and considering what future has on hold,
guy peeping is as good as any start.
There will be temples standing,
altars smoking, courts and palaces,

luxurious cities with noise and riot,
straw effigies in uniform,
glorious causes and bumkin barging in,
your *desaparecidos,* remonstrants,

rungates, refugees, D.P's
and those need answer for them
though they won't, kulaks,
subsidy men, moguls, sultans, lords.

Some have pitched their campaign posters
HERE, have dumb slogans
talking about the hard working people,
handwave for you, handshake for backer.

VIII.

Kid is back, not humming.
There is the post-stampede pile-up
of Calico critters on our bedroom floor,
lost narrative momentum.

Which makes me think,
in Herodotus, where there are fathers,
offspring, whole dynasties
but no children, where the sons

make fathers or mothers proud,
are citizens and heroes, how much
of the scattered is unaccounted for
in spillover, backwash, shards,

toys left behind in the gotta go.
She knows I'm writing her in a poem,
knows enough to question accuracy
and principle after she reads

because "that's not how it happened"
or "what it was," or "who did it,"
so will insert her own line here:
"She set up her calico critters again."

Though that was not my point
nor did it happen at all.
The lobster pot, the whine in the rigging,
the wreck and what washes ashore

which will make narrative only
if an opportunist comes to plunder.
400 ships lost to disaster and certain
Amenoicles sacavanged, sold the goods.

IX.

History is casting first moulds.
Rook, gudgeon, pushover.
Violento and tornado wait
for them round the corner.

Stray dogs orbit the camp.
Magi make up spells on the wind.
Eunuchs, female cooks and concubines.
Though particulars can make me

pause: the Issedones stew father's corpse,
save his head to guild and worship.
A bivouac of men shave their heads,
shearing the mane of a mule

just to get ready their lament.
Little oddities, yet to come
the oaths and twists in deals, shards,
what transpires in the second

a despot proclaims his "god of heavens"
and "by gods," which makes facile
equivalencies impossible as x is unlike
z if x stands for Raj and z for Rubicon

though there are fools involved,
and something nameless in us
for which each variable
is a smear of event right on the page.

Yet to come also Babur, crusade, New Deal.
Right here are history's building blocks,
strange folk, mean, clannish, squalid,
their idols wrapped in straw.

X.

So many roaming town to town,
not unlike the sort you see panhandling
outside a clinic or convenience store.
There's slave also, a constant in the math.

He has no choice but obey king, assuage
his insecurities. He crouches, hides
behind drapes, watches queen pull tiara off,
squatting in the sort of squeaky beam

that ends one dynasty to launch another.
She strips, slips off her embroidered tunic,
strews it on the ground, gets that feeling
of being watched, backs up. Vermin?

Burglar? A double-agent wad of cash
to behead the king and off her for a laugh?
Other wives will put up with husbands,
their apprehensions, braggadocios.

Other Kings will spy, spit-fire, curse the sky.
"By gods" they'll say in flood or draught,
"three thousand lashes to the River,"
subjects scurry like roaches to light,

begin to splash. This Phero fellow
forgets the river is a god, is blinded,
gropes ten years till oracle prescribes a cure:
"douse his eyes with the urine of a woman

who slept with none but her own husband."
History's early try at stand-up comedy:
He grabs a jar and rushes to the wife…

XI.

No yet yet, just future tense,
which is oblivion with a wash of types
your muckety-muck, or nabob or pooh-bah
with names, titles, offices. Khomeini anyone?

Cambyses? Olivares? Richelieu?
And now that nation state is as obsolete
as clan or jat, go update and add
the masterminds who came up

with petrodollars, derivatives,
hedge funds, going giddy over spikes,
shrugging away dips as they hover
like osprey over our lives,

while they purchase vassal states and wars
and make sure, no holds barred,
their mausoleum towers over
cenotaph, that anonymous survive

as off- the-cuff remark
that chalk-marks corpses
to the groundswell of the text.
One, epithet and epitaph,

"the sole survivor who came to a bad end,"
is as good as intestinal flora
in the convoluted telling of which he's part.
He backtracks to famines elsewhere,

poor shattered people, broken deals,
God took your hog but spiked your prayer.
Our fellow starts as hoplite,
fighting for his cause, what else?

XII.

He is full of bits of Homer in his brain
to sort out biremes, troops in full gear,
a whole epic clang of back slaps
as soldiers egg each other

to whatever soldiers egg toward,
a poetic justice that has it
the cheated-on get to trample on shark
and charlatan and double dealer.

What regurgitates is altogether different.
Call it the unpoetic clatter of hard fact,
a defeat our fellow headlines.
He rode on a histrionic wave,

drifted on the wake of defeat,
was plucked from the shallows
by women asking for husband, father, son.
To us their robes are chiseled rock,

their metalwork is in a museum case.
History being born,
relic isn't relic, and the guy
with at least one of its keys

is dripping, tired and unlocks each door
to a skeleton in the making:
the Jock is unburied; gimp unsung;
heartthrob's mutilated. The man living there?

"He breath'd his last."
The strange type who just hung around?
"His head was tossed among the throng."
Ten thousand javelins caught the light.

XIII.

And now my kid's third entrance
with a HearthSong catalog on hand.
She's circled stuff: lambs and assorted stuffies.
Here's what I'll fail to explain to her:

That there is someone always
with no qualms about his name,
christening the hangman's noose,
"part of the job" he'll shrug

that he's recruiting apprentices.
Ask what you will, object,
raise a question. From the top of the stairs,
he'll put on airs, know-it-all.

"You, down there
wait, go to your bar or games,
stick to a budget and don't go ask
for a face to face."

He is sure his is a burden,
whatever truth he think he keeps
with its cruelties and its realpolitik
leads straight to the fiasco

where mother's "told you so"
sheds its smug, prophetic knowing
for the sad know-how of survival
and where you'll find how mean survival is.

That metalwork in cases?
The women unfasten theirs to slit, slash
stab the guy with the rough hammered pin
as each asks for brother (bathed in his own blood).

XIV.

Fiancée? (a wound full on his neck),
friend (sleep eternal sealed his eyes),
till this survivor "perishes," Herodotus says,
and leaves it at that, leaves him bloody,

anonymous, tucked, a footnote to attire,
angry wives and low mobs, ready
to be washed out by something larger,
another host chanting slogans outside,

another mob making a point, the polyglot
of fist pump. Disbandings, re-gatherings
at trench or front, around another casualty.
Not yet the forced march, no Xanadu either,

History's cradle is a connubial bed.
Gyges, our slave gets caught peeping
and that will be his manumission
given he does what Queen asks—

be exposed and killed in a cover-up
or kill the king, be king himself.
Cradle and connubial bed
made of lust, what we sweat,

negligible frictions.
See the embroidered tunic fall,
its static sparks will catch history to birth,
will swell to bonfire where renegades plot

and light torches to pillage with
(pray kid won't find out first hand)
as they steal the flame again and again,
for triumphal blazes, pilots to infernos.

Folk

Like Bartok in the Balkans
with his wire machine
recording it all,
the landlocked yokels's lullaby,
Székeley tunes in Czík,
their vocal slides,
a shepherds' old church hymn,
the swineherd's ditty.
His longhand transcripts
don't miss a thing, either
pitch inflections, rhythmic tics,
reconstructing mother's keening,
excavating gunslinger's boast.
In the gamecock and fog
tracts where empires
grind down to meal,
the pipes and drums
are a press gang's tune,
the czardas fiddle rancor,
of the sort that
makes his music what it is:
simple melodies really
that in a hiccup show horn hilt,
brass pommel, the dagger in dance.

Political Animal

This poem has no politics in it.
People cast their vote.
There is in it an elected official,
a Sheriff strutting
like a would-be *cacique*
through something like a new frontier.
He's not the one in the news.
Though the off-the-record
small print benefice of office
and the invisible ink wrote
his ticket there is of a piece.
I want him at his cinematic best
with Wyatt pull on boots,
a Stetson in a train yard
not there to scavenge evidence,
meet an enemy or take bribes,
just scale him against late afternoon.
He is policing a county that's like
the country's *paysage moralisé*
with, on the one hand, boredom,
ammo rooms and anger,
on the other, nothing
at least during the working week:
three gateway Polo ranches—
executives fly in for weekends
to hang out with star or politician.
Ah, also the Mexicans that tend
and groom, stashed midway
between town and ranches.
He'll keep their volume down
and the townspeople know it.
They like the good boy done good

yarn even if some heard otherwise,
that from honorable discharge
to damned near untouchable,
the trajectory might've had
more than a few sordid stops.
Someone makes him as the bouncer
who disappeared from the scene
downstate few years ago.
A buddy of his has been herd tell
that he drives the red head and the Thai
on his cruiser to the mansion
where they lezzy-up for senator
in town and he is capitalizing
on the overtime and the discretion,
is getting tips on what cheap
fallow lands state is eyeing
for its principal industry these days,
pop-up presidios everywhere.
There is a parable here somewhere,
though none of this might be true.
I want Sheriff in the train yard
backlit amid grass and fence,
so much the makeup of America
no hinterland, no back wood
empty maybe but with major
congressional sway and pawns
turned venture capitalists
from nothing and with nothing
but obsequiousness and guns.
Freeze-frame him till sun sets,
sunset can swallow him whole.

Enterprise Zone

las banderas, ya sombras de Occidente
                    —Gongora

If not new squirearchy, our new burghers then,
the Korean clan accountable for most storefronts
on this block: the hole-in-the-wall Alterations and Repairs
where grandma sews; the wig and hair product shop
where patriarch oversees kin or brethren or accounts
or otherwise just dusts the dynastic set-up of styro-heads
lined up like cloned *l'inconnues* dredged from the foam
of packing peanuts and coiffured in bobs and fingerwaves.
They have the fruit stand also and the food cart
and the hybrid storefront selling phones and money orders.
Today, they've gone all out to promote the new concern:
a DJ, fifteen-inch PA speakers on tripods blasting house
as if this were Ibiza or the Keys. It's the youngest doing it.
The wind dancers sag a bit, corkscrew back up
like woozy crucifixions. The teardrop banners do
that millenarian thing Riefenstahl cobbled together
at Nuremberg, for the free market this time, like pennants
straight out of John Milton for Milton Friedman and his boys.
Look it up, Book I, the phalanx of banners when demons
wake and congregate. Why not? They've earned MBAs,
are calling the shots, with the G class SUVs and roadsters
they u-turn to parallel park right in front of the new place.
One of them is trashing the mascot, a girl in a pancake suit,
not keeping corporate identity, a mini-lecture on branding,
trademarks and how "no one, get it, no one is indispensable."
From home-spun and make-do, the entrepreneurial kids
have diversified, branched out and owe allegiance
to HQ's know-how. Our new burghers, as if hatched

from the gospel of our home-grown prophets—Rand? Hubbard?—
and strutting the part that mingles diasporas, pursuit of happiness,
the rise of capital, a muddled but sanctioned epic—
with banners, storefronts, and offices that turn men mean.

Invisible Hand

It isn't from the benevolence of the butcher, the brewer or the baker that we expect
out dinner....
—Adam Smith

The butcher, the brewer, the baker
or what Anheuser-Busch or other
corporate entities have churned
as modern counterparts,
bean counters, pencil pushers, CRM's,
Annie, Bob and Rachel
gather, listen to an insufferable
honcho—as they do for a living—
except they hope this sideline
will let them walk out on
the chicken scratch they have for wages.
The backdrop? A garage, that's right,
with exiled exercise machines,
cardboard on cement to blot oil drips,
a box for each holiday, five
for Halloween, collectibles, gadgetry
like an outtake from the evidence room
shelve on shelve, attest for debt.
Also our circle of foldout chairs,
a projector and a white sheet as screen,
nametags and literature like liturgy
waiting the more drawn out cast,
from a round of intros, to each other
and the guy on speaker phone:
Harvey is customer service rep
at Pet Boys, with enough seniority,
they patch him to the sort of caller
ready to turn plaintiff, "Packaging

was not as described." He "wants most"
to write sci-fi for the rest of his life.
For now he settles as Padawan
in the Jediist temple on Saturdays.
Nadine, a stay-at-home mom moonlights
at the Outback ("tips suck") keeps
an Etsy shop and wants more sensibly
to start a 529 plan, any leftovers
"a house down the shore would be nice."
"Anything's possible" guy on the line.
I'm always out of place, can't deliver
on the prompt, itinerant of sorts,
with PT here and odd jobs there,
hard to explain, came out of curiosity,
the wrong kind, and gave in as well
to a faint sense of obligation,
"want most?" God knows.
Pyramid scheme after pyramid scheme
they've invited me to every one,
the hosts. He did some pluming
for us, she babysat the kid a few times.
The conglomerate of lawyers on retainer,
a few years back, some Astroturf thing
a bit later, a wholesale website thing,
BurnLounge too. Today is "telecom,"
that's what Ken, captain, eighth ball,
stone polisher, keeps talking about
as he dashes through the Power Point
to let Joel, CEO on the line from HQ
at the Keys, "tell us a little about himself."
The anecdotes of success, failures first
like some repentant drunk "sharing,"

except it's ventures here not haunts
he touches on. Screen saver kicks on—
how long can he go on infinite iterations
of a nautilus Mandelbrot set?
Adam, an MT, who "wants most"
credit card debt be wiped, has a question
but Ken signals him to wait.
"Is everything okay there Ken?"
And now Adam's bait.
"Why don't we save the Q&A to the end,
Adam, and you answer a couple of things
for me?" Adam nods, Ken tells him to speak up.
"How much you guess I'm making a week?"
Ken's miming. His two thumbs spasm up.
"How much you think the watch I'm wearing
costs?" His cheapest one he adds.
"You know when you know?
When you're swatting the tax man away."
Then it's something about beachfronts,
where they stable the kid's horse,
"very expensive Saudi-owned colts."
Advanced math keeps casting
its psychedelic convolutions on the sheet.
There are chips and sodas.
I'd say if not benevolent,
patient butcher, brewer, baker;
I'd even venture and guess
what sets the table with their dinner,
what unseen mechanism
was more a machination
that blindsided them
out of their shops
to shrink wrap at Giant,
pipe icing at Shop Rite
and if capital have mysteries,
numinous to-do's, they're what

tap-roots in our last-ditch,
reckless grasp to believe in,
put up with anything.
Where's the wealth of nations?
In the egging on of thimblerigger
and shill, three card marmey,
cups and balls, short-con conjurer
and the invisible hand
which will pocket the money, run.
Ask the son of a butcher,
Mozilo, co-founder of Contrywide.
"Adam, ever heard of Patek-Philippe?"
Lest we forget the grandstanding
in the formula.
"No not really, eh?
Ken, why don't you do a search
on the internet." Tic-toc.com,
a page full of them.
"You see those prices, Adam?
Chump change to me.
I'd hold my hand up for you to see,
not that you could see it."

In the Russian Tradition

While the thaw's yellow wash swills
around horses, dogs, old men
left for dead to winter by the curbs,

the state will provide statistical truth.
Their kingdom come, a klezmery
Totentanz wears out its grief

for all, the stray, the malcontent,
the drunk, the fugitive, the son.
I'm listening. Before all that,

as proem to the slogans, mob trials, executions,
a math-wiz sulks over a chessboard
because last he saw Sophia on a troika

in someone else's arms.
Pay heed, the cast is well-spread:
The iconoclast is never in doubt.

Nor is his counterpart, the charmer,
the eccentric dressed to the nines
to captivate in ball and banquet.

Hard to tell the kulaks
country to town to peddle hoardings in silos
at the bar of the Imperial Club.

Elsewhere, the Khlysty and bonesetters
and bloodletters and midwives
with amulets and prayers for Vlas

the patron saint of cattle,
or Elijah, saint of flax and yarn
cast spells and forecast storms.

Governors burn or their effigies
in uniform—uniform being real.
The Cheka, the Duma, the Komuch

the Krug, the ministers of finance.
The prince fribbles, tsarinas and attendants
play tiddlywinks, as in that film

with its single ninety minute Steadicam shot
that hopscotches room to room,
back and forth three hundred years,

where, THE END, crowd descends staircase
to the final ball, it is the final ball,
the wound of the Red Army about to burst,

bleed what's wrong.
Our math-wiz is masterminding big
chunks of that future, weighing

the power of ideas, the errors of autocracy,
safe-housed in a toy shop,
smuggled to well stocked *dachas*.

He is in the music, undertone, thread
though liner notes say nothing of that,
go instead explain how Shostakovich

ciphered his initials to the score,
the coruscating harmonies
the serpentine, fiendish *ostinatos*

idée fixe, hang ups, Zhdanov
issuing his doctrines and decrees
a bore going match point against talent,

the macabre keeping time either side.
Again, of math-wiz, zilch
though he's the wing flap in

the butterfly effect that lets chaos in.
He's surly, pondering Q to her fourth
and Sophia, of course

in whose parlor slur a waltz here
or mazurka there as if to point
first, how quick the century's needle

skidded from the legato complacencies
of *guesten hall* to the *sforzando* of gulag;
second, in the furnace where domestic

was forged, how housewife was made
etude by *etude*, that there's venom
in the lovely and what it pretends.

That's why he's purging among *muzhiks*
abjuring pleasure, repudiating it even
but getting ideas with every explosion

the chessboard registers from far off.
Engineers are carving a railroad in.
That's right the Richter tremor

from each blow shifts self denial
to a higher cause, to be taken seriously
like a *Narodnik* charting nonesuch

which is violence by another name.
This being the Russian tradition, though,
he is being watched and those watching

are his friends. They'll turn him in,
eviscerate what right there is to his cause
and then invent themselves an office.

The Russian tradition has no place or end.
It's here and us, aftermath and aftertaste,
its high pitch *al niente* chord rings in the ear.

The Bosses

Guy walks into a bar, sits, turns to his friend.
Friend says, "How's the new boss?"
"A fucking bureaucrat," leaves it at that.

Boss having memorized the HR handbook
to the eleventh bullet point of a subheading
had just done his cut and paste job,

sent the email to remind and reprimand the staff.
But the friend is just nodding, guy shaking his hand
as if both where quick-sanded in the dream of reason,

or worse, had turned that sort of corner where
lurk the spooks on the prowl for poor schmos
in Kafka's world, specters of the system, or the system.

Another day, another bar, another schlepper,
standard issue rolling laptop briefcase.
Same question. "The boss?" "A fool."

This is no joke unless the joke is on us
nine-to-fiving it under archetypes:
the lout, the micromanager, the clown,

whatever style it takes to fuss and dissemble.
Anyway, this guy is here to drink, not scaffold
a third sucker come to deliver the punch line.

There will be a third one, still no joke—
fidgety, fatigued, shirt coming untucked,
a splice of middle age and come to think of it

the new Middle Ages too with fealties to lords
in office towers or corporate parks.
The master's corveé everywhere in evidence:

private elevators, golden parachutes,
heirs apparent to the new America
for which our fellow here needs only a hostess

to guide him to some booth in some craft beer,
tapas, gastro pub. He is running late.
No surprise. His day is at some boondoggle

where the principals do nothing, know nothing.
Peep into the cubicle where he's vying for promotion,
pictures of the kids buried so deep in paperwork,

a tesserae of Post Its with "remember," "to do,"
like an evidence map in a crime too tangled to resolve.
And that is just analog, with another more frazzled,

spread-so-thin version of the man in digital
if you unlock his phone, check his computer screen.
We've lost the symmetry of the joke,

its classical proportion, its three-part structure
and paperwork is not entirely to blame.
In his tousled prêt-à-porterish, post-yoga ease

boss is waiting for our guy in gastro pub
sipping from his green-chai hibiscus thing,
here to follow up on an email he claims

was very difficult to write. Yeah, run of the mill
Dear John stuff he follows up with consolation lunch
and small talk about the kids, the traffic,

while our guy peruses the seared and poached,
organic, local and other gibberish around a French fry.
Boss will have his regular, lobster paella,

then down-shift to explain why promotion didn't take.
Do we need to see the beast, his gaze as from the passing
bars, behind the thousand bars no world; the lout

inside his iron cage, a "nullity," says Weber.
Listen to him: "core competency," "tension in the system,"
"moving forward," "sea change," like a rusty weathervane,

noise showing where wind blows, new Middle Ages,
its *magnificos* and *grandees* sipping chai, a new America,
with micro-managers and bureaucrats and clowns. No joke.

The History of Wrongs

will take a while, doodle all you want.
Dot a pupil on each pearl stacked
to distraction on the margin. Argus froth out

a hundred eyes of which by turn did sleep
always a couple and the rest...
Scribble the obvious. *Life, friends, is...*

I cross-hatch around margins, a wattle tile
to while the crisis in the agenda.
He says: "We'll be tightening our belts."

He says, "doing more with less."
"I believe in we, we're all in this together,"
he says. Go fill in what riddle

you zone out to in the conference room
while you caricature their likenesses.
Aquiline or accipitral is it? He trains

on objection, a paper-chaser to his left
short-hands the minutes she'll send tomorrow,
a whipper to his right rubs her nose, nods to "we."

Vulturine maybe, considering
the missing bodies, vacant chairs,
the wake-like huddle just outside the door now—

an ad hoc, back-door meeting within a meeting
to slash-and-burn the operating budget.
The specifics are unspeakable,

(more ways than one) as in objectionable,
as in, talk, I'd be airbrushed out of history,
as in who can tell. In this shuffle and fudge,

caricature turns courtroom sketch.
Scribble the obvious beside the cluster of eyes.
They all go into the dark

the captains, merchants, bankers,
the statesmen and the rulers
(little consolation)

distinguished civil servants,
chairmen of many committees,
industrial lords and petty contractors

all go into the dark. Least worrisome
considering the body bags piled by statesman,
the banker's toxic assets, the petty developer

running for office, and the list can go on
while we attend another meeting,
hear one more transition team,

tune in to a press conference,
its obligatory, cutesy anecdotes,
fanfares to the common man,

the Joe Blow propped there to show
the man at the lectern can slum outside
of his *alma mater*, boardroom, club.

Ours here says: "The reason I was hired,
when they asked me, 'would you be ready'
I remembered, this cabbie, La Guardia

to Midtown, you know the type
I was going incidentally to another interview,
and I asked him, if you were me…"

You've got it, Jamaican fellow behind the wheel
clarified boss's call, defined his mission.
The gumption and wisdom of the patois

got boss this job and who knows,
comes time when gavel falls,
maybe even, will justify his means.

You know his type, CEO or CFO,
Provost, VP, administrator, screw
rushing from headlines and into the back seats

of town cars to get out of there
dispensers, directors, the *nouveaux* riche.
I'm getting ahead of myself, car pulling

away prematurely, though he will go
become "acting" something or other,
a higher post, then split elsewhere,

"a thrill and a tremendous honor,"
press release will quote, though we here
will only get a message from his boss

regretting the departure, thanking him.
Time being, he is in the comfort zone
of bound reports. "Any comment

or concerns? Just to make clear
I'm here to make this great place greater
and you're the way, wonderfully gifted."

He wants transparency and open doors....
Paper chaser cuts him short, whispers to cupped ear.
My friend Roy, has calligraphied his way

through the Chinese alphabet.
While they bumble for document
王八蛋(*wáng bā dàn*) bastard, son-of-a-bitch.

爛 (*làn*) crappy, lame, stupid , while they consult.
And 笨 (*bèn*) stupid, idiot, when he reaches,
he says, "the hard decision" and docks

in that rhetorical flourish where speaker stops
as if unable or unwilling to go on.
Pope—spent so long at the Iliad,

become a scholar in the sort of anger
come when bully, his unmerited rewards,
windfall profits, fringe benefits

short changes those soldier on for him—
calls it, the hem and hum,
the stutters and hesitation, APOSIOPESIS

"an excellent figure for the ignorant"
he explains, "as in *What shall I say?*
because they have nothing to say;

or *I can no more*, when one really can no more."
The grimace, the twitch, another whisper.
Net worth, salary, dumb titles, something

gives them the idea of who they are,
of who we are with scrawled margins,
ancient alphabets or ink stains to pass the time

they take to reach their nonplus, our cul-de-sac,
gather their papers, late for another meeting,
.... "any questions?"

No Fucking Rome

Quanti si tegnon or là sù gran regi
che qui staranno come porci un brago,
de sé lasciando orribili dispregi!
                    Dante, *Inferno*, Canto VIII

"Fifteen years, it's been fifteen years and…"
like a barfly who drives you to a corner
share in confidence or untangle frame-up,

the Ernie-looking fellow in the elevator
knows me from Adam but swoops
on me to mutter what grumble he had

going on his own as if to keep himself from
going postal, though it lands him back
in the dreary of so many "what nexts."

"I'm fifty, you know?" Short on ammo, long on scruples—
the difference between him and the "honcho bitch"
that handed him pink slip—he's left to chunter

and sort the how and why he's here
though he can't get past
the years of service, "fifteen years."

How many puff their way to the top
pretenders come believe they're sovereign for real?
Boss certainly does. In some idea of justice,

she ends up with the likes of her
to wallow for eternity in filth,
che qui staranno come porci un brago,

her doings here unspeakable, disparaged.
She's what head-hunter winnowed to come
straighten up the place, make it run.

"From where I stand these fucks are here
to dismantle the joint, sell it for parts.
She walked me through the handbook

I've been here fifteen years."
I have nothing to say. They browbeat their plans
into our day, call it legacy what barnacles

to institutional wreck or national memory too
if *corpus juris* and *corps diplomatique*
enter the record to be filed with all the other

sub sigillo workings of perfidy these days.
Perfidy is right, a bit Miltonic but right.
Word on the street, Ernie is the fifth casualty,

and word on the street is all we have to go on.
"I was the one who actually…"
Reader, you can fill in the blanks for him:

overtimes and clean-ups and good ideas.
HR still wants Ernie to turn in his ID.
They'll purge him from the system,

airbrush key codes and passwords,
something drastic enough, final enough,
upstairs, there is a lineup of loyalists nodding

every time she talks about how things
were done in the place she worked before
as if that were a sort of insight.

Why turn to crestfallen Ernie
who doesn't get it, is rueful, shell-shocked?
"I don't see why the other guy wasn't put

through the same ringer I went through?"
He's talking about criteria and double standards
about whether they deserve to keep their jobs:

"Two years here and what has she done, eh?
She wants 'transparency' she goes around
'transparency' she says but never lets on

as to her MO and what's with all this 'envision'
shit and that I'm not in the 'bandwidth.'"
"They love clichés and platitudes" I shrug

with little else for consolation, pinioned at the lobby
like an innocent bystander to gather what's
salvageable from wreck, hand it back to victim.

"They're 'rebranding" she said, and I came back
at her, you know what she said, she said
Rome wasn't built in a day. Seriously?"

We know how Rome was built.
Write an epic or have one written for you,
abide by its holy missions, its prophecies,

however many villages you scorch.
When in doubt, flip through it, eyes closed
your *sortes Virgilianae* thing, point a random passage

then fire your shot, call it a triumph, however off-target.
Because they go nowhere but up, theirs is perpetual
Interregnum, you are always interim,

spear carried with a psychic income
factored somewhere in their gambles.
"This is no fucking Rome, just look around,

it's not even a wannabee Rome with rotunda
and bust of the bully who endowed the place."
"They're more egalitarian around here," my joke.

"Egalitarian, not equitable." Ernie corrects
"and you know what else, ah, forget about it,"
waves me off, out the building, exits a final time.

The End of History

The same Parts, the same actions often promote Men to the head of superior Societies, which raise them to the Head of lower; and where is the essential Difference if one ends on *Tower-Hill*, and the other at *Tyburn*?
—Fielding

Everything is make believe: the mansion,
the garage, the office, the classroom and the planes.

On the other hand, the gag ball in the laundry room
is real and someone is going to get fucked.

So a guy, veins bulging, will grunt his way out
of a ludicrous plot while pupil or mother,

you get it, list whatever fetish you want
from the not so *sub rosa* argot

that sweeps though MILF, plushies,
incest, facefucking and hentai,

and there is no need to spell out the dénouement.
Free markets or libidinal economies

what's the difference, go split hairs,
one's Juggernautish momentum

gathers midget, ugly, cheerleader, cuckold,
frotteur, the other keeping captives in Patpong

or Kampthipura, recruits in Florida
with adds on Craigslist to cast

its public or real estate sex, stranded teens
or the cougar who walks in mid-coitus

to chastise stepdaughter but joins
the teens to teach the boy.

All preposterous down to the camera work—
free market, libidinal economies—

their scenarios, what's real or make believe.
But pause, there is allegedly a larger plot

in the guy, vein bulging,
since where I read about him or it,

file or video is encoded with bit parts
of a larger conflict, an *addendum*,

article implies, to the end of history.
Read here, not the *Diaes Irae, Tuba Mirum*

last syllable of recorded time kind of end,
worst, a sort of po-mo, neo-con concoction

where it's bye-bye Lenin and all that
and to all that, dismantle Great Society,

say no more to grand narrative,
let manifold that rolled over vistas

to tame and conquer them stonker,
throw in a sput satellite for laughs,

rig lost its teleology, plants shut down.
Put that way, but for the camera noise

the end of history is not unlike it's birth:
the bedroom farce, male gaze prurience

as empire scrambles, a constant in the tale.
Like the beginning, full of dissipations,

their aftermaths, *Villa de Miserio*, *Tugurio*
with the R&R of *Zona Norte* or Pataya

the *panem et circenses* for the disenfranchised
Dirty Latina Maid, Hijab Porn, Gonzo, Indian.

They all have their categories in any free porn site—
go look, the castaways at end of history.

There are other abjections, caravans on foot
with the skimble-skamble of few belongings,

going around lands fenced in for redevelopment.
As I said, not that different except for

the heavy machinery involved
the mile on mile of environmental graphics

to cover up whatever bombinating chimera
is churring at, churning in the fosse.

A bit more secular, the end, more on the line
of capital and its invisible hand visiting

of all places, all places, to open up
or crack them open, set them free

so more portentous, with an agenda,
like the angels that visit Sodom and Gomorrah,

except who's there to tell corporate
knocking at the door what Sodomite tells messenger:

"Angel? Bring me an angel so I get to know him?"
Meaning, he'll do to angel what guy onscreen

is supposedly doing to the Sarah Palin lookalike.
Yes another plot, though to put on the side

since whatever is encoded in the video
has nothing to do with the parody

or its politics but with the more paranoid
IT nature of what we miss.

This here, *Nailin Palin* a five act beginning
with Russians and a knock-knock joke,

moving through the studios of Bill Orally,
to finish with Serra, Hilly and Condi in a ménage,

or at least a seized digital copy of the film
could render Lyotard or Fukuyama wrong,

since it might have the meta-narrative we lost
encoded, encrypted through "steganography."

"Security through obscurity," Wikipedia says.
A technique that rigs the pixels in an image

zero distortion, slips something like underpaint,
which if you know, have the necessary software...

"The art of secret writing" says the OED
in the less mangled, more *longue durée*

lineage that would let Histiaeus in
just to get, if not a sense of continuity,

then "more of the same," one more mold
Herodotus cast. He descends on Chios

like a plague, lands a settlement in Thrace,
commands enough resources to worry

the guys in charge, his souzerains.
No need for context here, familiar enough,

your run of the mill satrap, "summoned"
by his betters who know he need be curbed.

Being who he is, he manages to wangle
his way out of sequestration by stirring

a revolt back home, manages to invent
a way to smuggle intel pass the brass:

shaves a slave, tattoos his scalp, waits hair to grow,
dismisses him with one directive

get home, shave, bow down.
Same idea, except, in high-tech, skim

the least two significant bits of each bit
component in a photo—I'm still wadding

through explanations, waiting the main point—
Zebras grazing in the savannah,

a selfie, the coliseum, it doesn't matter,
you could hide, Hamlet, Macbeth, Othello,

both Lears full text and that's Zebra
being King's misprision. With a video

at thirty frames per second, you do the math.
The point being they found the metanarrative

in porn, some clash of civilizations thing
because what better place than snowball

kitty avatar to tell those in the know
go "bomb" and how many recruitment vids

can you compress while Palin's lookalike....
Talk about "more of the same,"

the prurient undertow that daubs
the conspiracist forecasts of hawk and pundit,

the misread signs or oracles, fools getting
everything wrong, budgets, strategic plans—

"Don't fence the isthmus. Do not dig.
If Zeus wanted it, he would have willed it."

They can't tell ground from figure
or maybe it's all the background noise,

the heavy machinery involved, wellbores
sounding for shale gas, offshore platforms

and accounts, the clubby, inner-circle
handshakes that make Jada Fire

as Condi nose dive on sleaze factor.
Sure, names aren't as clever:

Philip Graham, Alan Greenspan,
Hank Paulson. Remember Cassano?

They're all in Wikipedia alongside
a full article about *Nailin Pailin*.

So just to make clear, in the making
of this poem, I've seen no one get fucked.

Of Biblical Proportions

Genesis 19:26

I mentioned her elsewhere, the pillar of salt
a literalist somewhere claims was radioactive
foam from a nuclear blast the Lord rained on people.
Their debauchery, the limits of no limits.

She, told to pack up, go, to not look back.
And Moses, Moses prophet, Moses zealot,
Moses indignant at the golden calf, Moses
if literalist is what we want, reigning in

the ancient equivalent of a refugee camp
where loyalty, let alone faith, back and forths
to what chirms from tent to tent. He knows
the odds in forced marches, Moses does,

the confederacies, conspiracies and cliques,
also that blow of a hammer, drive of a bat
instant in the looking back, the decency to turn.
It isn't about home, not even about longing

though a literalist says she must've harbored
neighbors' sin, was complicit, compelled.
Really you just have to figure what the guy
next door is up to. He doesn't have it coming.

An affinity, not an alliance, knowing
that injustice comes down as law
and pity the arraigned, stumble a moment,
the fire and brimstone, the burning plains.

Moses vicar, God's man and man of God,
can't have what's learned in the look back,
but he, lawgiver, teacher, can't do a thing
except excise her name from the account.

Winners of the Saturnalia Books
Poetry Prize:

Telepathologies by Cortney Lamar Charleston

Ritual & Bit by Robert Ostrom

Neighbors by Jay Nebel

Thieves in the Afterlife by Kendra DeColo

Lullaby (with Exit Sign) by Hadara Bar-Nadav

My Scarlet Ways by Tanya Larkin

The Little Office of the Immaculate Conception by
Martha Silano

Personification by Margaret Ronda

To the Bone by Sebastian Agudelo

Famous Last Words by Catherine Pierce

Dummy Fire by Sarah Vap

Correspondence by Kathleen Graber

The Babies by Sabrina Orah Mark

Also Available from saturnalia books:

Sweet Insurgent by Elyse Fenton

The True Book of Animal Homes by Allison Titus

Plucking the Stinger by Stephanie Rogers

The Tornado Is the World by Catherine Pierce

Steal It Back by Sandra Simonds

In Memory of Brilliance and Value by Michael Robins

Industry of Brief Distraction by Laurie Saurborn Young

That Our Eyes Be Rigged by Kristi Maxwell

Don't Go Back to Sleep by Timothy Liu

Reckless Lovely by Martha Silano

A spell of songs by Peter Jay Shippy

Each Chartered Street by Sebastian Agudelo

No Object by Natalie Shapero

Nowhere Fast by William Kulik

Arco Iris by Sarah Vap

The Girls of Peculiar by Catherine Pierce

Xing by Debora Kuan

Other Romes by Derek Mong

Faulkner's Rosary by Sarah Vap

Tsim Tsum by Sabrina Orah Mark

Hush Sessions by Kristi Maxwell

Days of Unwilling by Cal Bedient

Gurlesque: the new grrly, grotesque, burlesque poetics
edited by Lara Glenum and Arielle Greenberg

*Letters to Poets: Conversations about Poetics, Politics,
and Community*
edited by Jennifer Firestone and Dana Teen Lomax

Artist/Poet Collaboration Series:

Velleity's Shade by Star Black / Artwork by Bill Knott

Polytheogamy by Timothy Liu / Artwork by Greg Drasler

Midnights by Jane Miller / Artwork by Beverly Pepper

Stigmata Errata Etcetera by Bill Knott /
Artwork by Star Black

Ing Grish by John Yau / Artwork by Thomas Nozkowski

Blackboards by Tomaz Salamun /
Artwork by Metka Krasovec